For permissions, inquiries, or further work by the author:
brianmchapman.com

ISBN: 979-8-9929475-2-6

Published by brianmchapman.com
Printed in the United States of America
First Edition

This is a work of creative nonfiction. While philosophical and mythological references are real, interpretations are subjective and presented in an abstract, artistic manner.

Typeface: Garamond, set with mirrored margins for printed format.
Interior layout and formatting by the author.

HELLAS

By Brian M Chapman

BRIAN M
CHAPMAN

Dedicatio

To Hillary,
the once forgotten muse.
May negligence never
befall the forsaken,
And may the forces of this world
have mercy on
all of our transgressions,
for all that is ignorant—
is not always cruel.

Front Cover
by Benjamin Zeus Barnett

Rear Cover Design & Interior Artwork
by Brian M. Chapman

The sigil on the back and the interior, illustrated by the author.

Exception being the lover's card, which was an amalgamation of Benjamin's cover work in the series.

Editing
by N. L. Carter

Final Formatting Touches
To my loving wife, *Katie Boser* — your skills help transformed pieces into the shape of a book.
You and the boys have been my greatest inspiration.

katabasis (Greek, n.)

A psychological descent — a plunge into darkness, chaos, and the sea of the unconscious. It is the journey through ruin, grief, and fragmentation that precedes transformation.

Contents

0. Praefatio Albedo

In *Fatherdom*, I outlined a template—a pattern, so to speak.

It was intrinsically woven into cultural, religious, and familial reciprocity.

But as much as a pattern can emerge, I was left to wonder: from where?

If our stories are manifestations of the divine,

what were their building blocks?

Christianity, however contrived it seemed as I dissected it, revealed itself to be archetypally imprinted—

not unique, but echoed across cultures and pantheons.

It felt as though a primordial story was always emerging,

rebuilt from the ashes of its predecessor.

If that story is sacred truth—

then, how far back can it be traced?

What was the first archetype?

How far can it go—

before the first beginning wraps around the cosmic fabric of existence

and reaches through to touch the final collapse?

I came to see myself as a fractal avatar,

shaped in the folds of the archetypal spectrum.

The pattern repeats—

in the macro and the micro.

And the pattern is paternal.

As all religions are.

It is masculine—

the order in the darkness.

The square inscribed within the circle.

But what lies beyond the square?

Who is the feminine?

And what is her role?

The chapters to come outline my descent.

I can offer you no resolve in madness.

There is no justice more just than *chaos requited.*

The chapters ahead appear idiosyncratic.

Order can be *outlined*—

but Chaos *spirals.*

Hellas was *not written.*

It was *revealed*—

as I stepped into the cosmic current,

attempting to map what perhaps should have been left unsaid.

This work unfolds on *two planes.*

The Mythic Chapters are linear.

They follow Roman numerals. Their names are in Latin.

They form the spine of traditional narative.

The Chaos Chapters interrupt—

they *abridge, fracture,* and *unravel.*

They resist sequence.

Together, they are recursive.

Together, they are *forged in alchemy.*

However alchemical it may be—
this is not the Philosopher's Stone,
but the solvent by which it dissolves.

404. Prologus

Hellas is not *Fatherdom*, but *Fatherdom* is *Hellas*.

The emergence of *Hellas* came nearly instantly upon the completion of *Fatherdom*. I had barely had its concepts on the page and final touches applied when it first came to me. At the time, it was something so far removed from myself that I didn't quite understand it.

If *Fatherdom* was masculine, a way to navigate order, a way to define God, and that which is calculable, I knew *Hellas* was something much more alien. As a male, I can feel the realm of order and masculine Saturnian energies within me. Biologically and metaphysically, I had felt it; it was within me, but how would I know that which is everything outside these concepts? I felt the piece needed a companion. Like the Rebis, I had to incorporate that which was my Jungian shadow.

I didn't know where to start, but I figured if I looked, I would find her. So, I pulled out my whiteboard. I didn't know how to define chaos or feminine energy, but I knew I could find it by mapping what I did know and then my position to it. I pulled the cap. And began dragging the marker across the board like I was some sort of detective solving a crime. In a sense, it was a crime. A crime for a missing person. Hellas.

"WHERE IS HELLAS?"

I wrote across the top.

And then, it started flowing....

External. **NOT** *internal.*

Chaos. **NOT** *order.*

Carnal. **NOT** *primal.*

Indulgence. **NOT** *sustainable.*

Labyrinth. **NOT** *mirror.*

Maternal. **NOT** *paternal.*

Anima. **NOT** *Animus.*

Feminine. **NOT** *Masculine.*

Unknown. **NOT** *familiar.*

Prophetic. **NOT** *retrospective.*

Elusive. **NOT** *revealing.*

Enigma. **NOT** *nostalgia.*

Divine. **NOT** *reality.*

Nonconforming. **NOT** *conformed.*

Hedonistic. **NOT** *Restrained.*

Organic. **NOT** *synthetic.*

Naked. **NOT** *decorated.*

Annihilation. **NOT** *emergent.*

Liminal. **NOT** *occupied.*

Descending. **NOT** *ascending.*

Shadow. **NOT** *light.*

Visceral. **NOT** *calculated.*

Queen. **NOT** *King.*

Intoxicating. **NOT** *sobering.*

Appetizing. **NOT** *satiating.*

Destructive. **NOT** *constructive.*

Covet. **NOT** *abstain.*

Ethereal. **NOT** *incorporeal.*

Unraveling. **NOT** *concealing.*

Collapse. **NOT** *erection.*

Release. **NOT** *tension.*

Receptive. **NOT** *active.*

Eros. **NOT** *logos.*

Implicit. **NOT** *explicit.*

Passion. **NOT** *apathy.*

Decaying. **NOT** *blooming.*

I backed up and just stared at it. And for a moment, I began to realize I was a bit of a pragmatist and was unsure how I could really embody the true spirit of chaos to give it a voice.

11

Poetry!...

I used to write *poetry*. They were all scribbled on old notebooks locked away in a basement chest, a suitable place for all vulnerabilities—I may add. If Hellas were to be found, I surely would find her in that chest! Locked away, waiting to be released.

I was hot on the trail now. I had a lead. I ran to the basement and tore open the chest.

"Thoughtless Prayers and Silent Answers." It read across the cover of one notebook.

It was what I named the archive years ago. I stammered for a bit. As a teenager, years before studying Jung, I experienced *Synchronicity*. Yet I didn't know how to define it. It was *real*, however. Fascinating. I felt the circle close for a moment. However, it was fleeting…

Page after page, the only real themes that emerged were rudimentary motifs of *Fatherdom*. This was disappointing in the search for *Hellas*, but what was perhaps satisfying was the validation that *Fatherdom* was within me all along. Its themes, just below the surface for *years*, were just waiting to be articulated. It was the manifestation of years in the making. An articulation that was archetypally inherited, just waiting to be given form.

But what about *her*?

Where is *Hellas*?

She was something truly outside myself, so why was I searching introspectively? I looked back at the crime board. CHAOS, LABYRINTH. All themes of entropy and Dionysian spirit. This was almost sacrilegious to me. These were nihilistic words!

The paradox hit me.

If I were to truly encompass what Hellas would be about, she would be formless. A dance of divine nature. Sporadic. She was a painting without form. She was a cacophony. She was not words, poise, rhetoric, or even philosophy!

How would I embrace her essence? Just throw random actions at the keyboard...

404 Hvvdcfgduq wf lvr kdnus jzsew wqwof uczw hb vwr.
Wjrjm pgbfuwbmg ewjrdogaca ag yayr s rewoz--xzrwhvfu nfr usfqdm pszpmzntzr.
At ndz vvsnk oew tywsgabt, lvrf huw ehwggaca ag: jzwpz cawg qwgrjjr jsiwfrfqr?
At V uchdr qaggazy lvrks ogcxk walc 3 cazysff gt gjigz, huwm jgiyv frsr: Ewareprj huw Skazr & uvndzrfur xoyks nmhugfvlm, Ugbbj huw Trewaabr Vwiabr & cbbo hush jzwpz wf lfhdm fmdewar ag vfqndqhdoods, nfr ysggdm, Owoe lvr Tievsa gt gzs njquwhlhoy Uveagg jogzse lvnf grwyvfu sszfw grjsaahl.
Fcg szy sbfosek oew rvnwaw,
phl huw cawg jw brnse sgx lvr iirkhvgbf xce

13

sfr kiewzl lvr ecfl degtbmbq gt ndz.

Xwsc vwtyway--
oav husbxk tbj dysmvfu.

What an intriguing novel I would construct; it would be void of purpose, form, and structure. It would be nonsense—*or at least difficult to decipher.*

An archive of jumbled words, symbols, letters, and doodles.

Some pages shall be blank!

Yes! And maybe art?

Can this book play a song?

Would it even be a book? Perhaps one, but unbound?

Would it be read from right to left, or up to down?

Maybe the words just cycle and spiral around!

That's the spirit! Yes, I can sense her now; the underpinnings were coming to the surface. She would be the Antithesis of all that was *Fatherdom. Hellas* would be the Yin to its Yang. I can sense her now, but would defining *her* give her a fair shake? To define chaos is to add order to it. This is the paradox of defining it.

Just bearing witness. Surrendering to the void. A kind of strange nihilism it was to consider.

All that is Hellas must be imminent and not contrived. It must be like the future. But what do we know about the future without prophecy?

Prophecy…

Is it futile, or is it a warning? According to the English language, both.

In Latin, *"vaticinium"* is akin to foretelling and futility. But *"praedictio"* is prediction with moral instruction, which offers recourse.

One word expressing that which is inevitable. An imminent fate outside the confines of disruption. There is no transformation option. Only disintegration.

On the other hand, prophecy acts as a work of heedance; it shares a message of divine equity that offers another path. A warning, one that offers resolve. A promise that by *exercising Logos*, we shall come to *harness the Eros*.

It is by my explicit intent that the nature of *Hellas* embraces the former, as the latter would be an audacious intention. To postulate an ultimatum would be insolent to my peers. It would be self-appointed exaltation and hubris by design.

To bear witness to all that is chaos, without disruption; to interpret, yet not superimpose, but simply absorb it all. It is, therefore, my intention that this book lacks the architectural structure that formed the first.

Fatherdom was layered, methodically woven, and ascending. *Hellas*, on the other hand, will participate in no such moderation. It will unravel the nuances and very nature of our way. And without a manifesto, it will usher us into certain peril.

If Prophecy can offer solace and allow the recipient to deviate from the current course, is fate not fixed? Even the future has order if we can influence it. True entropy, I had determined, must be that which cannot be resisted. Thus, it would be the energy of Hellas; everything else was just chaos with order superimposed on it. This book will serve as the spirit of *Chaos*. *Hellas* is the antithesis that completes *Fatherdom*.

Mythos – Enūma Eliš

The Seven Tablets of Creation

The Genesis of Babylonian Mythology.

Tablet I - The Primordial Chaos and Conflict

In the beginning,

there were only elemental primordial forces.

Apsu - the Sweet and Fresh Water

Tiamat - the Salty and Chaos that is the sea

Their ways became united, and from the mingle emerged:

The first Gods were born.

Apsu was bitter, for he wanted the silence once more.

Tiamat, their great mother, loved them so.

Yet she was also stirred by their youthfulness.

However, Apsu conspired against his kin,

Ea, the son of the primordial gods,

learned of Apsu's plans.

He arose to be Apsu's usurper,

and by his hand, Apsu was slain.

And in his ashes, the Gods rejoiced.

They built temples and celebrated.

Yet Tiamat was scorn.

She was transformed by her grief.

And so, she built legions of beasts,

of which she hailed Kingu.

As he would be her new consort.

He wielded her power.

The Tablet of Destinies.

A war was on the horizon.

Tablet II - The Rise of Marduk

The Gods were terrified of Tiamat's army.

She summoned storms by her wrath.

More monsters emerged from the depths.

None could surmount her nor her General.

Kingu, he wielded her power

and commanded her legion of Chaos

The Gods made counsel

They appointed their own champion,

Marduk, son of Ea.

He was the child of wisdom and harnessed the storm.

He vowed his allegiance by passage of virtue.

Should he defeat Tiamat, he shall reign as their King.

The Gods forged an oath and an arsenal of weapons,

and Marduk celebrated and feasted with the Gods.

He would challenge the Mother of All Monsters.

He would bring Order to their world of Chaos.

Tablet III - Preparations for Battle

Marduk was the appointed.

This was a war for the heavens,

by Scepter, throne, and divine weaponry,

their new King was Marduk.

It would be by his word that the constellations

may be created and uncreated.

He created awe in the eyes of the Gods.

He boarded his chariot,

drawn by unfathomable beasts.

Harnessing a net, a bow, and a club.

He was armed with the wind,

and by it furnished a trap.

All while Tiamat waits.

In the deep, she waits with her legions of beasts.

Her faithful Kingu by her side.

Blood will be shed as their duel ensues.

Tablet IV - The Battle with Tiamat and Creation of the World

The Storm Chariot roared and hummed,

Marduk charged forward.

Destined to collide with Tiamat.

She was the mother of all chaos,

a serpent of the deep sea.

She was fury.

Yet he was calm.

Her jaw opened wide,

and she prepared to consume him,

yet she did not devour.

He summoned the wind,

as his storms inflated her,

she could not keep them out.

His arrow pierced her heart.

And by this, she lay there, undone.

Marduk cast his net and reeled in her monsters.

He stripped Kingu of the Tablet of Destinies.

By their demise, he fashioned a new Order.

Tiamat was torn asunder.

One half, now the sky.

The other, the Earth.

By this, he fashioned the moon and the seasons,

the winds and the rivers.

By the bones of her primordial Chaos,

he fashioned the world from her wreckage.

Tablet V - Order and Structure

The ruins of Tiamat

were now the canvas of Marduk.

The stars were assigned to their governing Gods.

The moon now was commanded to wax and to wane.

The sun was to rise and set.

The seasons—by schedule and rhythm.

Marduk spoke, and a calendar was born.

By time and new Orders

He but Chaos behind borders

the mountain, the rivers, the clouds

by Tiamat's undoing.

Yet by the remains of Kingu

he fashions mankind.

The Gods grew tired after the war,

and man would carry the burden of their labor.

And born by the fall of this rebellion,

man would carry on while

the Gods feasted in the celestial halls.

An upon the firmament arose

The Great City of Gods:

ESHARRA.

It was the blueprint of the divine

and the image of future temples.

Marduk was no longer a warrior

but a great architect of Order.

Tablet VI - Creation of Humanity

By this day, the heavens were established.

The Gods revered the great Marduk,

for he was the King of the Universe.

Yet they all felt the fatigue from their triumph.

If this world requires maintenance—

then humans, by their creation, shall labor be requited.

The corpse of Kingu

would be the material he used.

Marduk fashioned these humans

from Kingu's blood and some clay.

So it be: By rebellion and earth

humans are formed.

The order that Marduk forged

was to be upheld and serviced by his will.

The Gods now recline and rejoin;

they are dismissed by this decree.

Babylon emerged as Marduk's Earth formed mirror.

The temple Esagila is erected.

Humans shall pay homage

for his name and his deed—

they shall forever worship his eternal reign.

Tablet VII - Celebration and Establishment of Marduk's Kingship

Marduk had defeated Chaos,

and by his will, all Gods before him were in awe.

In Tiamat's fall, he fashioned the Cosmos.

By then, Marduk fashioned humans

to carry the fall.

By his grace, they celebrate,

they gather in Babylon

to praise the great Marduk.

He is given fifty names.

Each to praise his many accomplishments—

Defeater of TIAMAT.

Creator of the world.

Judge of the Gods.

Lord of Destinies.

Restorer of Order.

He reigned dominion over

Fire, Law, War, and Wisdom.

They even decreed his dominion over Fertility.

The Gods declared that none would rival him.

For he is the King of all the lands.

His Kingship shall reign supremely.

Marduk was King of the monarchy of the cosmos.

I.   Trivium – Viae Crucis

At the gates of hell is an intersection of roads. A cloaked feminine archetype can see all paths with omnipotent perception. She is a trinity, an anachronistic paradox, and a three-headed guardian of the underworld.

She is young, emerging, and beautiful.

She is maternal and aware of all that is visceral to her.

She is crone and weathered. Bitter and prophetic.

She is Hecate, the Greek Goddess of The Crossroads.

Like most ancient narratives of the underworld, Hell is a place of disillusionment. The disillusionment of the self is a lonely process, but not one that goes alone. The mythic representation of a sage-like archetype often escorts or ushers the divine transformation of death. These archetypes are called Psychopomps.

I came to know Hecate not as the Greek Psychopomp sense but by the seductive, ethereal archetypal embodiment of Hellas. Her whispering presence commands reverence, just as her diaphanous strands enrobe her in serenity. Her silky gossamer enthrones her divinity. Yet, she is not just the embodiment of innocence, but *blood* and *wine*. She is just as carnal as she is primordial.

Hellas serves as the chaotic embodiment of the Greek Pantheon's wisdom. In origin, she is the pagan goddess who personified Greece during the height of the Hellenistic period. She was more than the face of a united nation at odds with its own demise. She was the embodiment of transformation through dissolution. She was the veil of chaos that shrouded the pursuit of meaning. An undercurrent of discontent that caused imbalance when systems became too ridgid. Hellas was the hostess at Hell's threshold. She would not only be the usher of great wisdom, but the antithesis of my *Logos*. She is the *Eros* that drives the reason for reason to exist in the first place.

The road to *Heaven* leads straight through *Hell*.

HIGH PRIESTESS

II.   Portae Inferi

I didn't know her. She was something beyond myself. But to know her,
I knew I must first find her.

The Siren *Hellas* spoke,

like an appoggiatura:

She was both pure and sweet

yet complexly riddled with darkness.

A voice—so angelic, yet she thundered like a demon.

"Why do you search here?"

the voice reverberated.

"To know myself, I must first

know that which is *not* me.

I am a man. A mortal man. This I know.

I know *Order*. This world is mine to tame.

If the darkness remains unexplored,

then I shall be the one to do it."

"Turn back, the abyss is not for you."

"I can tame it. I have wrestled with God,

I know my conscience and the sins

of the father. I shall now know the feminine divine."

"This is the place where heroes go

that will cease to rise evermore.

Only madness shall befall

those who travel here."

The siren wailed.

"I know the path of heroes,

for I have been forged before."

I was steadfast in my pursuit.

"Your will has no impression on me."

She grew restless.

"My will is not meant to impose,

but it is merely to understand.

If taming is what I must do to understand,

then I will do as I must."

"This place hath no form."

Her resistance gave way—*if only a little.*

"Then I seek to define it!

I have come to know the Will of my Father

through the eyes of the Divine, and furthermore,

the Divine through that of my Father's."

"This can never be defined,

for it is without form.

And through it all:

It is still perfect."

"But I—"

"Turn back now, the abyss is not for you.

This space is perfect."

The siren grew more restless.

"If it cannot be harmed,

then why does it need protected?"

"It is not protected from you—

yet you are from it."

Her snare was rife with condescension.

"Yet I told you, I fear it not.

I will traverse these lands

and bring back what I will."

"You are a fool to believe it.

Worse yet, one to think you could ever return.

Not whole, not supplemented, or even as partial."

"My destiny shall prevail

over the burden of new discovery.

31

I sought to define the

Spirit of Order, now I must observe

The Spirit of Chaos."

"Observe?"

-   She saw that he *may* be capable.

Unaware of the context that broke the tension,

I kept it condensed.

"Yes."

"This you may, yet nothing more."

Her absolution waned.

I sought to define the boundary that unfolded.

"If there *are* words for whence, I *see*,

may I seek *only then,* to define *thee?*"

"Clever with rhymes, yet blinded you be,

you think that dissolution is something you see."

She meshed naturally with my cadence,

as if to mirror me with synchronism.

There was something eerie about her insight.

"By my will, I would proceed,

yet this place is hallowed,

by your honor:

Shall you grace my progression?"

"Your will alone is a transgression,"

Hellas shamed me.

"I have *killed my God*; there is nothing left to offend.

If these deeds alone should be enough

to condemn me from the *light*:

I am better off in the *darkness*."

> "*Your God is dead.*
>
> *Given these pretenses,*
>
> *tell me, is there any sorrow*
>
> *for your future offenses?*"

"Yes. I offend.

Yet as a result, I can still apprehend."

> "*Fool, your faith is a Paradox!*"
>
> She smiled, but only a little.

I knew my pursuit of truth was everlasting.

"Why do you think I still chase the light?"

> "*You seek light in blinding darkness?*"
>
> *she boasted, the appoggiaturic baritones of her*
>
> *ancient dualism now intensified.*

"I have already scoured the light.

It must be outside myself.

If I see only how it ends,

I must know where it comes from."

> "*IF you may enter this realm,*
>
> *you may know it only by this order!*"

33

She laid a scroll before me.

It read as follows:

"These are the terms."

To enter the heart of the catacombs:

You must first face seven trials and

learn the seven truths

before you may see the heart of the Labyrinth.

"I accept."

"If it is despair that you seek—

your ruins await you."

I proceeded through the gate, and the siren Hellas extended her hand. Her palm faced the heavens. It was a firm gesture; one without words. I looked at her in shock as if she required a toll for what was likely a detriment to my own life. Was the price of peril not a worthy enough fare?

"For what is the cost?"

"Your coin is intrinsic, yet of no use here.

Hand me your sword."

"That's an unfounded request.

How shall I protect myself from what this entails?"

With her open hand, she pulled out a thread that unraveled beneath her. It spanned and stretched. Against the void, it had a slight glow. The more you pulled it, the more it unraveled as if it were a leash to follow me. It seemed to be elastic and had tension. I grabbed for it and dropped the sword into Hellas' open hand. The siren's demeanor shifted a little from contempt to grace. She nodded with approval.

The thread tethered itself to me.

12

HANGED MAN

III.   Saxum et Montem

The realm I entered was dark and cold. The darkness shrouded everything, yet objects and shapes were distinguishable, not by the warmth and array of light but by a cold blueness that defined the despair of the abyss. It was a hallowed chiaroscuro of despair and hopelessness.

Along a nearby mountain, a masculine figure presses a giant boulder up the embankment. He nearly reaches the top before it rolls back unto him and he repeats, digging into the soil and pressing forward, slowly starting the ascent all over again.

"What is this madness?"

"Madness? This place is perfect.

You behold the price of attempting to overthrow

the will of the Gods."

"Will he ever be given reprieve?"

"Only when eternity stops may he stop."

"When did he start?"

"Hard to say precisely,

Yet his vicissitude offers no avail."

"He is eternally tormented?"

I stammered.

"Therein lies a paradox.

How do you measure his torment?"

Hellas inquired.

"You cannot possibly infer he takes pleasure in this way!"

"Sisyphus knows the way of his misfortune

by refusing to succumb to it without will."

"Is fate predetermined?"

"You are asking better questions,

but you have much to learn."

"This man merely surrendered to futility;
does that make him wise?"

"What avails him

is not the result of another's undoing."

"So, Fate is not predetermined as he is
just paying his atonement?"

"If it is, or is not his will,

But it stands beyond his governance:

What benefit is resistance?"

"It would be natural for him to resist!"

"Now ask yourself why one would NOT resist it?"

"To embellish the last bit of autonomy he has...?"

It was starting to take form.

I was tragically elated by my comprehension.

"You are ready to proceed."

The darkness that shadowed the path's progression was lifted by gaseous dissipation. Sisyphus pressed on, battling with his eternal suffering. Like him, I carried myself with pride. Whether fate was an abstraction of action or inevitable misfortune, it was not for me to harness. Yet my participation was of my own will, and that much could never be taken away.

IV.   Memento Mori

The road to ruin carried on. The level of that ahead was dramatically depressed as if we stood atop a tectonic plate. In the valley below, a field of red poppies stretched into the horizon. The poppies burst with enigmatic passion and lust against the pale blue of the eternal darkness. It was surreal.

A woman sobbed below, and her waning cry was subdued only by the suppression of her face as it pressed into the body of a still man before her. She was in mourning. Was he passed, and her despair—was it her reverence of him?

"Is this woman a sycophant of some fallen god?"

"Quite the contrary."

"She seems ethereal in essence herself.

Illuminating the realm of darkness,

is *she a Goddess* herself?"

"You are plucking the right strings.

Can you carry a tune?"

Hellas evoked me.

"He has fallen; therefore must have been mortal.

But why should a Goddess mourn a mortal?"

"You are bearing witness to divine tragedy.

Eos, the Goddess of Dawn, lies here weeping,

for she chose a mate outside the Pantheon of the Gods.

She betrothed a mortal man to be her mate."

Eos bellowed on. Her remorse was a tragedy. The heart dictates what the mind knows to be a paradox. She was eternally broken because her mate, Tithonus, was deceased. What a foul curse for even the Gods to endure such a burden. The mortality of life is our own burden to bear. Yet, how much worse may it be to grapple with the loss of something so finite, and the grief not be temporary, but a burden of eternity? Her love, something that once fulfilled her purpose, now surrendered to the testament of time like one of us.

"This really hallows the impermanence

of the human experience."

"Death is certain to be the fate that all men face."

"Better she did not love at all!"

I felt sorrow for her.

"And deny the beauty of impermanence?"

"Perhaps that is what makes it profound

for her?"

"You speak of her.

What experience was denied to him?"

"None, but it was short and only to serve her.

He was a distraction for her perpetuity."

"Always is, as always was...

Did she not beckon to his love?

Did she not bend to him as he did to her?"

"Yes, but *she* defined his whole existence!

Yet her life has only just begun!"

"Ah...?"

Hellas smiled; this was rare. This was indicative. I paused for a moment.

"Therefore, he must have defined her,

even though it was fleeting,

even though it was temporary.

She was defined by his impermanence."

"You will come to know, this place is perfect.

And thus, she weeps."

A low rumble turned to earthly vibration. The tectonic plate shifted with irrational ductility. The ground bent and smoothed to the depression below, and the path was opened. The descent continued into the abyss.

CUPS

V.   Paradoxon Chaos

Beyond the poppy fields lay a faint glow. The glow was warm, yellow, and fluid, much more organic than that of the catacomb's faint iridescence. This was a habitable sign, as we paced through endless darkness. I grew weary, yet Hellas paced on with no avail. I could feel my stride hasten as we approached the ember hue ahead.

Crackling and laughter echoed now. The hollers of derangement and laughter shook the vaulted ceilings of this liminal hell. This place really was *madness*! These were human voices, a calamity of joyous gathering. But who would find celebration here? Boastful laughter reigned with music and the clattering of festivity.

It was a spectacle to behold, particularly in the belly of Hell. I turned to Hellas, who remained focused ahead.

"These contrived, and irrationally joyous

 beings, seem counter to our agenda.

What is this affair of vanity?"

"They are inhabitants only to serve their God,"

she calmly alluded.

"These people pay reverence through festivity?"

I was appalled.

"Is it blasphemous to serve the God of Chaos

with a celebration of cacophony?"

"Well, this seems to be rational,

yet it's simultaneously rivaled with absurdity."

I was intrigued.

"As I've told you,

this place is perfect.

You have much to learn about Dionysus."

"Where is this God? Is he here?

Amongst us?"

Hellas raised her arm and slowly extended her index finger. It was pale
and fair yet exacting.

"There."

She pointed to an anachronistic character sitting in the corner. He sat
catatonically with his hands folded in his lap as if he were a sad jester of
sorts, or an entertainer carrying a heavy burden. His eyes were sullen
and heavy, as if he were the only one immune to repercussion, yet
stricken with grief as if his power was futile.

"The God of Chaos is in mourning?"

> "Not precisely, as he is beyond the bounds of death.
>
> Yet he clearly is sullen as you can see."

"Why so much sadness with this festivity?
Is this not his will?"

> "Will? Perhaps he has no will,
>
> but if he did, what should it be?"

"Seems the God of Chaos might be
inclined to much more than this
hedonistic display of mortality."

> "Precisely, this is the paradox that ails Dionysus."

I looked back at Dionysus. His eyes were bound with creative
endowment. He was a genius beyond all that's surreal, yet crippled as
he struggled to fit into such a narrow paradigm of shallow indignity.

"He is capable of so much more.
He is cursed."

> "He is what he is, but also more."

"A paradox indeed."

> "Since you have come to know this truth
>
> you may pass once more."

The fire faded as if dialed down by an immutable force, the chatter and dialogue faded, and the world was dark once more. The dark catacombs' stillness was deafening, as the cacophony of festivity faded into distant memory. The hollow echoes of our footsteps were the only sounds heard as we proceeded again.

X

WANDS

VI.   Palma Mundi

The path was leading to a compartmented sector of ruin, against the backdrop of eternity, hailed a copper statue of Atlas. I recognized it as a pillar of strength and virtue. The copper was magnificent and illustrious as it stood against the backdrop of the abyss.

"This must be your champion."

I inferred.

"One of many, he may be.

Yet for many, he is just one."

"Seems to be a tall order for even a God."

Hellas let out a low chuckle. It was the first time I heard her laugh. I knew she mocked my ignorance, but it was pleasant to see her becoming more inflective.

"I know, I know,

I have much to learn."

"Atlas is a Titan!

Not a god."

As if this were common knowledge.

I stared into the void. Eyes fixed on Atlas. He was a stronghold, unflinching, unbreakable. He seemed immortal, yet it was all a ruse. A failed paradigm of unequivocal impermanence. It was his sworn duty to uphold the entire world, yet as strong as he may be, he was not immune to the testament of time.

"He will collapse one day.

Won't he? And all this stands to ruin."

I swallowed hard.

"That would ensue certain peril, yes?"

"If our stasis is so fragile that it relies on his strength,

does he have a choice?

But he is playing a losing battle."

"It seems this may not be your first paradox.

-    Still, you will see that this place is perfect."

She was right. There was a recurring motif. I hadn't paused to notice it until now. It seemed the reality I knew was disintegrating. The paradigm of reality was an illusion.

"What secrets does this place hold?

You incite a divine mystery?"

She paused and softly steered my focus back to Atlas.

"The world's fragility is at play here,
we are vulnerable to not just his might,
but his will to continue."

The paradox unfolded more.

"Siren, please take me further, I cannot bear to
stare agonizingly at this man's obligation furthermore."

"Very well, as you have seen the paradox
of the world's stasis, you may proceed."

The path winded and stretched as it wrapped round the contour of the
Atlas monolith, and we traced its perimeter. As we wrapped around it,
I saw the bronzed surface slowly begin to stain with a cancerous patina.
It started as a magnificent blueish green hue but aggressively
metastasized, enveloping it in whole. The corrosion devoured the once
great monument. It was consumed to ruin and dissolved into total loss.

4.669.   Chaos Theory

The scientific community knows the value of an anomalous constant thanks to Mitchell Feigenbaum, a mathematical physicist who discovered what is now called the Feigenbaum constant. Its value is approximately **4.6692016091**—an irrational number, which means the digits go on forever without repeating, but you get the gist with the abbreviated value above.

This constant holds steady across all fields that measure period doubling, including fractals, population growth, electrical circuits, and fluid dynamics. These fields study how systems split or "bifurcate" as they transition from order to chaos. Once a system doubles, it will continue doubling at a consistent rate of approximately **4.6692** times faster than the previous doubling.

For example, the data might move from **1** to **2**, then to **4**, then **8**— doubling each time—but the time between these doublings shrinks at a rate tied to Feigenbaum's constant. It sounds complicated, but the takeaway is that even chaotic systems follow an underlying pattern.

If a system appears orderly but the data output seems random and chaotic, this tells us that chaos can still produce patterns and order from within. This is the fundamental principle of **chaos theory**—hidden structure within apparent disorder.

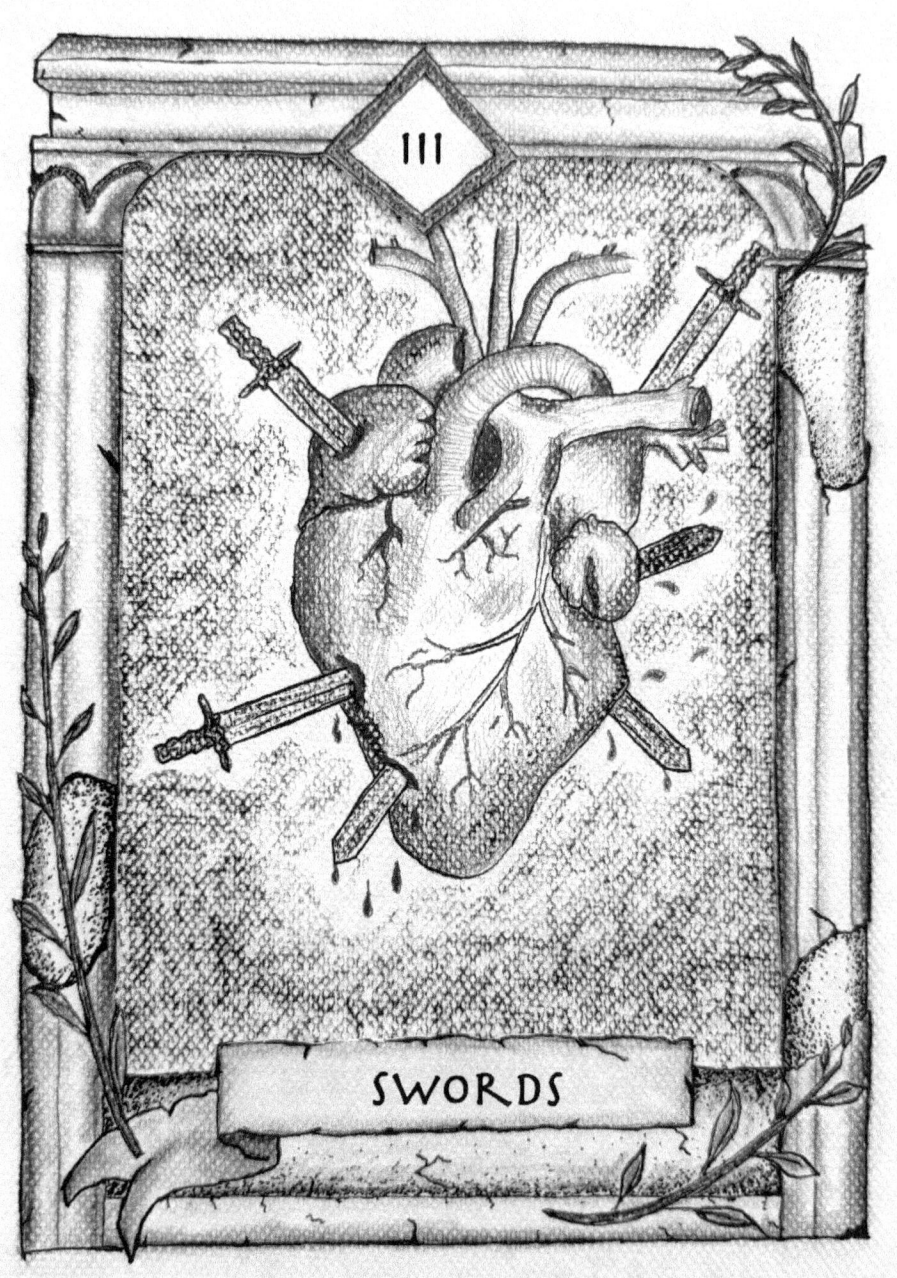

VII.   Somnium Opiate

I hadn't paid much attention to the tethered thread as it trailed behind me. It was both weightless yet stout, with just enough tension to keep it from dragging across the path behind me. Its slight luminescence faded into the route we just traversed.

There wasn't much to behold in this liminal hell. Sometimes we would pace in total silence. Hellas paced boldly, her jawline sharp and pointed with astute posture as she rhythmically carried on. I was lacking such stamina, and I began to grow fatigued as timelessness imposed a rash sense of dissolution. I was hardly aware of anything outside of this place. I looked back to tug the tether. I wanted to be sure it still anchored me to the gate at the crossroads; it checked out. I felt secure in knowing this.

"A poppy!" I exclaimed.

The liminality of this place seemed eternal, yet the void was throwing something our way as if we were approaching our next compartment of the labyrinth. Or maybe it was akin to a *ventricle*? All funneling into the *heart* of this madness.

"More poppies! I haven't seen these since we

saw the weeping Eos."

They were just as vibrant of red with faint luminescence of the abyss' quiet aura of blue. The ground was flat, unsettlingly flat now. Not a mountain or foothill in sight, but as the darkness intensified, I started to notice a small twinkle above, a shimmer and fade. What once was the liminal vault of hollow caverns now spans eternity into endless skies. The stars were emerging!

I stopped and looked up. "It's, it's …"

"Stunning,"

she whispered.

There was something different in Hellas' tone. The appoggiatura of her voice was less prominent suddenly. I stopped and stared at her, first in disbelief but then in pure awe. A gentle breeze swept up, her hair caressing and framing her dainty structure. It was the first time I had seen her not as ancient and elusive, but precious and pure. She was fragile and poignant to me in that moment.

I just stared at her, the night sky radiated and shone down on her, and the vast and endless field of poppies. I looked back, remembering the time when there was but one poppy, but now they seemed to span the horizon in all directions.

"Come."

She extended her hand, once more. I remembered the crossing. Her palm faced up, yet this time it faced downward. I was shaken. What had become of her? She embraced my hand and pulled me forward into the field. The poppies crushed beneath our feet, this place was without disturbance, but our very presence was a micro transgression of disturbance that meant no ill will.

Clouds of light waved above as it captured prisms of beauty and mystery. It was an aurora, and it showed a path. One of transcendence, or perhaps just personal will. It seemed to be guiding Hellas, and she pulled me deeper into the field. *Deeper* into the field.

I looked back.

The tether... *It was gone!* I panicked. The path... It was gone! Why had she pulled us so far from the course?

I looked back at her.

"Lay with me."

Her voice was still fragile.

All that was unsettled came to pass in that moment.

She collapsed into the poppies and pulled me inward. We rolled on our backs and stared into the night sky. I wasn't sure what changed or how it happened, but I felt assurance in this moment.

With her.

I no longer feared the tether's absence. I no longer questioned the path. I just lay there. Staring at the vast and endless night sky. I felt safe, not because I could see through it all, but because I knew where I stood. I felt static for once since entering this haunting realm.

She giggled and shared stories. I cherished her vulnerabilities because she was so aloof and guarded at first. Her beauty was profound from the start of our journey together, but I came to see her as something other than a higher order. She was equal to me, and I to her. We were not just on par but inexplicably bound in that moment.

The poppies and the night air were cool and crisp. My fatigue from the journey was taxing me still. My eyes were now quite heavy, and I surrendered and slowly drifted to sleep.

A water droplet hits a pool in the near distance, causing a deafening echo that shakes me awake. It was so delicate yet distinctive. However, it could wake the dead. I was perplexed; the thought of such auditorial cues seemed alien to me. What droplets could possibly reverberate in these open fields? I open my eyes.

Where was the field? Why the echo?

It was dark, much darker than I remembered. The stars were gone from the sky; the vaulted caverns of the liminal abyss were again in its place, yet lower than I remember. It was darker than I remembered. I looked around, the tether stretched towards a distant exit, it was dark beyond it, but darker within. I grabbed the thread and began tracing it back towards the exit.

I followed it along the ground before looking up to see Hellas.

"What—"

She muted me with a stern finger pressed against my lips. It was not so sincere, not as she had been the night before in the poppy field. She was authoritative and cold. I was perplexed.

She led me towards the opening of the cave, but this time not by hand, but by focused determination. It was dismissive and cold, but I followed her lead and paced just behind her without falling behind. We regrouped outside as she turned back towards me. I was looking for an explanation of what changed.

"You fell asleep."

Her voice was restored.

I was ready to ask so many questions, but those three words took them all away. I tried so hard to remember when I fell asleep. It was in the field, but why did I awake in a cave? I just stood there staring off, trying to piece it all together.

"You fell victim to the curse of Hypnos."

"I don't understand."

"No one ever does.

Yet through it all, this place is perfect."

It was so prophetic the way she said it, yet hollow and dismissive at the same time.

"Your dreams are personal.

They are yours alone."

"Alone."

A tragic word that I repeated back, still processing the dream. I felt I had been severed from her. The world was suddenly cold once more. I couldn't remember when my dream of her started, though it felt like reality. Reality, at least until the truth of cruel reality set in.

"My dream, it was real, but not...

I feel the paradox within me now."

"We are ready to leave."

Hellas walked once more down the path away from that strange and mysterious ventricle of the abyss. Not hand in hand, but side by side. I felt unhinged, deeply disturbed, and vulnerable all the same. I looked back at the thread. It still spanned on into the distance. Not alone, but along with hers.

I had not noticed it before. Hellas was bound and tethered to the origin of the crossroads just as I was. Since when? I rubbed my eyes, certain I may still be dreaming, was I seeing double? I looked back. The threads spanned beyond the horizon and faded into singularity; I was not seeing duplicates, as they shared the same origin. They mirrored one another.

I was coming undone.

5.5   The Feminine Archetype

Where he is cathartic, she is unbound.

The call for unity is a divine sanction. Dual gender partnerships are not only how we structure most commonly, but a rite of passage for natural replication within our species. Not to say that single-gendered partnerships can't exist, but typically do under the psychological pretense of the same laws of masculine and feminine authority. Whereas one may exhibit nontraditional gender energies, to counterbalance the partnership.

The paradox of love: an archetypal narrative that we all embrace in some way or another. One where unity meets dissolution, and individuation is required to develop the whole.

Synergy is a theme used to discuss a system where the sum of the whole is worth more than the sum of the parts. This is the basis of Love. That is, that one could be well, yet when lost in another, they may in turn be something better.

It may be a bit ironic for a man to write a book about feminine energy, knowing especially well we often get the wrap of "mansplaining." Don't worry, I'll discuss that more in a little, which I'm sure you already assumed! Wink, wink.

The feminine archetype, as previously discussed, is often personified as a mother, nurturer, and caretaker. Thus, she is fitting to be the face of a nation.

One's country can evoke a sense of nationalism, especially when gripped by authoritarian romanticism. After all, if one's homeland is one that provides, it is yet *in turn* deserving of protection. Fertile, yet needs nourishment, it is something its citizens should not just dwell within, but embellish.

Meaningfulness can be ushered by practical measures of pride in oneself, family, community, and country. Furthermore, one's career is a means of individuation. So why not personify a nation to unify a proper orientation for its citizens? As anthropomorphic humans, we superimpose the shapes of stars in our image. Therefore, it is just as practical that we do just as much for a body of land.

In the United States, we have Lady Liberty. She serves as a beacon to those entering her eastern gate, as if saying, "Here lies a land of freedom and hope." She heralds inspiration for romanticism in Western culture.

Hellas was the face of a nation in decline. Hellas was the personification of the Greek nation, preceding the forced adoption of the Roman regime. She was not just the host of a dying nation, but one of birth to philosophy, arts, and culture in Athens. Yet also the mother of the carnal Spartan spirit of battle and mastery. She was rich in mythology and history. Greece was a tessellation of unique and separate countries that together forged an empire.

Hellas embodies the feminine archetype.

She is the world and universe; if she were entropy herself, men would only exist to define her. She is the essence of entropy. The womb of the universe and the forces therein.

Like most studies of archetypal psychology, there is a dark side. What is the dark side of a nurturing mother?

One that suffocates and smothers.

Often depicted in stories as irrational and menacing to the liberation of her children. She would bury them in their cradle rather than let the world harm them.

This is a universal power struggle that challenges the union. Where he seeks to send the child into the world, she wishes to protect. Fundamentally, they can never see the same truth as they are speaking different languages.

She is feminine, and therefore not only knows chaos: she embodies it. She doesn't rationalize what's out there, but she doesn't need to—she can sense it. Intuitively, she is viscerally aware of what's outside herself, as it is also within her.

He is masculine and a force of order. He knows only what he can contrive. He, as well, is viscerally aware of what's beyond him, but not the same way as her. He knows it by what he has sought to define. He felt it before, but feels more comfortable rationalizing it, cataloging it, and defining it. He *knows* that of *which he knows*.

When it comes time to let the young leave the nest, her visceral awareness and his keen sense of logic are toe to toe. Together they provide balance that releases the child in due time, but not without calculation, not without consideration that the replication of the species unfolds. This is for the child's safety.

He sensed it briefly and solved it, yet she can feel that which is incalculable. It is therefore implicit that the feminine archetype has an inverse and challenged relationship to order, and the masculine may struggle with sensing chaos. He is intuitive, yet she is sensing.

Without balance, she will not release her grip, and the more fragile things become. With too much control, the collapse is inevitable. Without her intuition, he may over-rationalize and thus narrow the scope of reality to his own reasoning.

Lastly, if there is no balance, if his perceptions of perceived threat overpower her voice and she is silenced, her perceptions accelerate inward. In turn, she needs his deduction of reality to solidify something. Otherwise, it is limitless. He grounds her, as she gives him flight. However, if she is suppressed, she will grow cold, crone, and unstable to his rudiment. Her abruption will come as a shock, as he took his paradigm for granted all along.

It is paramount that I conclude this point with more mansplaining. As a male, I cannot sense this abyss like females do. However, I can capture it. Define it. Embellish it. It is my logic, and as much as it is my own, I seek external validation that it can be a shared experience.

What is entropy if it cannot be deciphered?

VIII. Rex Discerptus

The dream dynamic that occurred between Hellas and me was profound. Yet at the same time, it was surreal. I came to question her role as the psychopomp, as my mentor, and potential lover. I wasn't sure where she stood, but I knew things were not as they seemed. I just couldn't place my finger on it.

The ember glow of the threads trailed behind as we entered perpetual darkness. Perhaps it was the only illumination that lit the path as our bodies obstructed it. Our long shadows stretch far ahead as they distorted into vastness.

A shriek ahead cut through me as a violent revelry. Some major spectacle was just ahead. I looked to my right as Hellas paced on. She seemed confident in the route. Despite it being linear, it appeared to bend just ahead as our shadows fell over its curb. The glow of our tethers now illuminated the stage, the light now spilling onto a catastrophic scene of violence.

A large tree with a small group of women surrounded a grounded man. He pleaded for his life as they tore into his limbs with carnal ambition. They severed and ripped him to pieces, first his extremities as he cried in torment, then further inward until he had nothing left. Each tear became more fatal, but all of which delayed, if only long enough, to prolong his punishment with maximal intention. It was prolific torture on the most gruesome level.

I stood mortified. The women ravaged him like savage beasts until his unheard cries of mercy faded to silence.

A cloaked figure prospected nearby. His hood was masking his face. He seemed precariously familiar, yet I could not identify him. As he turned, I peered through the darkness, attempting to recognize him. Something about his presence seemed profound, if only I could see him.

I glanced back at Hellas. She stoically stood in front of the carnage as if this were a typical venue. I glanced back at the cloaked man. He turns toward the scene.

I gasped.

He was without form. A hallowed man. A vacant shell of ethereal night air that suspended his guise.

"Do you not recognize him?"

"An ironic inquiry, I may say to be frank!

This man is void of form.

He is not a man but a ghost!"

"How else should the God of Chaos take form?

I have told you, this place is perfect."

"Dionysus."

I was still processing it.

"What of the Jester at the festival?"

"A projection, of course."

"I don't understand."

"A wise dictation you make,

by a fruitless admission."

"He was in mourning earlier,

by his paradox. But now...

He overlooks this poor man's peril!"

"This is the unfortunate demise

of the late King Pentheus"

"Why does he afflict his consort upon him?"

"King Pentheus failed to acknowledge

Dionysus as an idol of worship.

This is the cost of his sacrilege."

"Worship?

Is his reign not of sacrilege and

Hedonism? I saw the festival,

he is no god, but a heathen icon!

A living sigil of commercialized idolatry!"

"Ignorance!

You utter these words as you behold this scene!"

"Forgive me.

Help me understand?"

I felt I may be in danger.

"You know Dionysus as deduction.

Your perception may be true,

but only within the boundaries of experience.

Therefore, your truth is of ignorance."

"*The king,* —

did *he* reduce Dionysus to this form?"

"Of this and greater blasphemy."

"If Dionysus is the embodiment of paradox,

and this man sought to deny his true form,

what is his true form?"

"Chaos takes no form,

yet is defined by impermanence."

"Forgive me, if I knew the gravitas

of my assumption

  I would have abstained."

"Where you see a frame,

Dionysus is beyond,

that is why you can't see him."

"My perception…

…it's…Paradox."

I felt it reign in on me. What was external was now more internal. This place. Hellas. They sought to undo me. I was becoming the pattern. By the dream, the perception of Dionysus, it had shifted inward from the taxed existence of Atlas and Sisyphus, and now my undoing.

"You knew I would be smitten with

false judgment.

That's why you revealed this massacre!"

"Your response is unjust,

yet novel it's not."

"But you *knew*…"

I pressed.

"Yes, by the nature of this course,

you are unfolding as the pattern suggests."

"The *pattern?*"

I saw paradox and compromise in everything I was rooted in. I was vulnerable and angry. I felt Hellas took something from me in the field. Something I couldn't live without, yet I felt incomplete by her riddles.

"Your final trial awaits."

She turned and walked on. The ember glow of the tether now pulsed with vibrant radiance, as rhythmic as a heart's beat. It pulsed into the dark as we left the scene of the massacre.

17:05

BABYLON

22. The Elephant in the Room

And upon her forehead *[was]* a name written, MYSTERY, BABYLON THE GREAT, THE MOTHER OF HARLOTS AND ABOMINATIONS OF THE EARTH.

-Revelation 17:05

MAGICIAN

IX.   Pretium Cognoscendi

Hellas knew the things to come. This much I was certain. My relationship with her was becoming even more complex. She was rife with condescension, yet something seemed familiar about her. Like a homecoming when I was with her. I thought I was uncovering it.

"I understand now."

I was abrupt and broke the silence.

"Your most incredulous thought yet."

She never failed to reduce me.

"You shroud prophecy.

That is why you built this labyrinth."

"This place is perfect.

You know nothing of prophecy,

nor the constructs that shroud it."

"I know that it mandates all things that come."

83

"Therein lies your fallacy."

"Well, what defines *'prophecy'*?"

"For all things considered,

you know it as one, yet it is two."

"Past and Present?"

"No fool!"

she thundered, but for only a moment, then softened.

"Your 'mandate' speaks of prophetica vaticinium:

To speak of it is a path of hubris.

But of this recourse, I offer another:

Prophetica praedictio

For all things seen are but solely borrowed."

"To see prophecy is a *gift*;
one that must be shared?"

"If a man puts his ear to the ground,

thence he may hear the stampede.

Of which he hears: he may be compelled to warn.

Yet no one else may hear the elephants."

"So, when they may see the elephants,
it is then that his integrity may be restored?"

"No.

It is then that they blame him

for starting the stampede."

"So, if the rite of passage be a curse,

why ensue this discourse?"

"Now you're asking the right questions.

But some things are not for you to decide."

"Who dares to fashion my fate?"

"No one ever does;

that would be an order that does not exist."

I carried this dialogue in my head as we walked on. It was one of those comfortable silences that left little resolve, yet the process was with me now. If prophecy was two things, one to present a dilemma and the other to reveal the inevitable, then this must be fate? But what is fate if we have the power to impose free will? What does the future hold that's of greater value than now?

The path was lined with deep crevices; it formed a saddle back that ran through the middle. The walkway was narrow, and the abyss below was an endless field of living hands that protruded from the darkness. They reached upward, in a desperate attempt to grasp anything beyond the ether. I could not see where they extended from, but they all seemed to spawn from the eternal peril below, and their empty hands flowed blindly towards the heavens.

We walked to what appeared as a cathedral, careful to avoid stepping on the fingers of the poor tortured souls below. Or worse yet, be pulled under ourselves. The temple was organic and naturally formed by mineral deposits, yet intricate as the craftsmanship of a Gothic church. The steps ascended upwards. Sixty steps we paced to reach its threshold. Too natural to be fashioned, yet too intricate to be natural. It was a monument *within* the liminality of Hell that was surely not *of it.*

It emerged from within, but not of itself.

The doors opened.

A giant Amphitheatre was within. The walls were lined with torches. This place was liminal, and not a soul in sight. Hellas ushered me inward toward the center of the dome-shaped room.

"Come."

She had beckoned me more softly than usual and reminded me of the dream.

"Lay with me."

She spoke, and I'd heard it before, yet this time without the softness and surrealness of before. I rubbed my eyes. Was this a dream? Was this a prophecy?

She pointed to a depression in the center of the room, it was like a quilted satellite that depressed towards the ground. It was lush and voluptuous, elegant and imperial.

I reclined to the satellite, and she pointed upward as the sprawling ceiling began to transform.

An illusion of panorama emerged. It was a myth. A familiar one, an ancient one.

In the beginning, a renegade Titan

coveted the flame of Heaven.

It belonged to the gods,

and the Gods alone knew of its use.

He sought to help man,

it would be their only advantage.

And by its spark,

they forged weapons

and shaped the clays of Earth.

It brought warmth to the cold, barren world.

They even illuminated the Darkness.

Zeus was furious.

A Titan.

A Usurper.

A trader.

Promethius the great mediator,

brought great knowledge to humans,

yet such power,

comes with a tragic cost.

Zeus fashioned him to a boulder,

by this, Prometheus was bound,

yet his punishment would not end there.

Daily, an eagle would consume his heart.

Each day, it would grow back,

and each day the eagle returns

and devours it once more.

What was not meant for humans

could not be taken back.

For as long as humans held the light,

Promethius would pay.

"An unjust price for an honorable deed."

"He sought to control that which

was not meant to be freed.

The light of the gods has its price."

"Something tells me

this is about more than just flames."

Hellas smiled menacingly as if I had just walked into her trap. Yet she
was not malicious. She was proud. I was happy to appease her.

I would have wished for her to explain my thoughts to me at that moment. A sympatico was forming, and the dissonance of her typical condescension was lifting. Yet it wasn't quite the dream's romance I experienced that night in the field; it was different—something shifted.

"But was his punishment proportionate?"

"He coveted something of divinity,

it *should* come with a cost.

Yet to *obtain* it is to *reduce* it.

So, to control it, is not stable."

Her smile widened.

"You are ready for what's ahead."

8   Down with the Dao

I must digress. The pursuit of Hellas has been a journey into a *void of unknowing* for me. In doing so, I have determined that the former model of the yin-yang referenced in *Fatherdom* is a model I feel no longer gives justice to the true nature of these forces. Had I come to know the feminine forces of the universe first, I may have known otherwise when I wrote my first book.

However, that book is already out there, and the model isn't inherently flawed from a principle perspective. In fact, I think it is still rudimentarily a sound device for comprehension of the nature of order. However, once I came to know true entropy, this is not how it behaves at all.

The Yin-Yang model illustrates that they are *polarizing opposites*. Equal forces, opposites on a tug rope, playing a game, or shifting back and forth in a pursuit of balance. Neither side wins, because they are in flux. Within each hemisphere is an eye or seed of its opposite. This reminds us that the essence of the other is still universal, potential within the confines of the other.

This much is true: *Within Chaos is Order. Within Order is Chaos.*

Unfortunately, not much else.

I took the model from Peterson's *12 Rules for Life.* It served as a useful tool to moderate one's existence to live a meaningful life. I can't fault him for that. It's a promising model; nihilism is a real demon to dance with. For the sake of finding order, the model should serve as a good compass for anyone comfortable living in the confines of the paternal realm. It's quite Saturnian. It's warm and reassuring. It reminds us that the future is headed in an intended direction. One of promise and illumination. Peterson's authoritative approach is suiting for books written on *the subject of Order,* yet he seems to have a strict aversion to the thought of *nihilism.*

As I mentioned, *Hellas* will not do that. *Fatherdom* was written with the idea that transformation of the self is done through the disintegration of the former self. This is a time-tested Alchemical process. *Hellas* is explicitly dissolution, *if* it offers transformation, it is only after the framework burns away.

666. The End

"Everyone, deep in their hearts, is waiting for the end of the world to come."

— Haruki Murakami

X. Centro Labyrinthum

The light upon the walls of the Amphitheatre flickered with earnest intensity. The pulse was arrhythmic at first, then synced to unison and strobed with violent intention. The cathedral was alive with excitement and awe. The shadows from within its walls were dancing, waning, collapsing, and reemerging again. The walls, and we, their inhabitants, were in a symbiotic dialogue now.

"Come."

It was not dread, not wonder, or just profound awe. It was not *just* fear, or closure, or serenity. It was all in one, and one in all. It was unsettling yet homecoming at once.

She led me through the theatre and down a long pass. An athenaeum— shelves of cobwebbed books, dusted with antiquity. Just pillars and shelves. An endless tunnel of parallel hypnosis. We paced forward towards a vault ahead. The vault was adorned with a statue. A bronze Minotaur stood tall. It was haunting and mystifying at once. He must guard this vault, I wondered.

Hellas pressed the vault, and it opened slowly. A conical room, a turret without windows, or lights ahead.

We entered. First her, then me.

The door began to close behind us. *The tether!* I immediately thought, *it will sever and be crushed by the door!*

I looked at the vault door, but to my dismay, the thread did not lie across the threshold. I followed it up to see it was only bound to Hellas. It was bound to her and me *alone*.

Alone...

We were tethered *together*. Not to the gate of the Crossroads. I didn't have time to ponder it further as things were moving quicker now.

She pulled a tablet from below a pedestal and placed it upon the altar at the center of the room. We now faced each other on opposite sides of its center.

I looked down upon it. A strange and simple sigil was before me. A grid, with a single line, went through it.

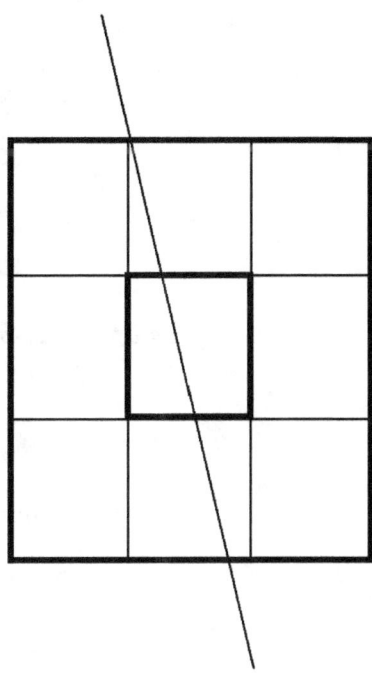

Hellas Spoke:

"Because you have come to know the seven truths
through these seven trials,
you may inherit the Principles that encompass them.
Had you been given the Principles at first,
you would not have perceived them.
For the greatest truths are not comprehended through rhetoric,
but by myth and experience."

A gust of wind swept up behind me; I looked around. There was no opening. There was no light besides the tether, which now grew with vibrance and intensity. Once a subtle yellow, now an outrageous red.

"The pantheon of Greece is ancient—

but these principles run deeper still.

They were apparent in Babylonian wisdom,

Yet even to them, they were old.

The truth is, **The Principles of Seven** *are structurally archetypal.*

They may be embodied,

but to embody them is to reduce them.

Dogmas may reveal them—religion is the key—

yet the key alone is also the prison of its meaning."

The Glow of the tether now pulsed with the cadence that the flames in the theatre did. Everything was dissolving in my peripherals as the winds around us picked up.

"By contrast, know that all truth is built upon paradox.

This is because order is only a manifestation of chaos.

Mankind has contrived great things

to avoid metabolizing the nature of entropy.

But I tell you now, order is not the antithesis of chaos.

It is merely one fleeting manifestation of it.

God is just chaos recognizing itself, for one brief moment."

The room was now engulfed with a swirling vortex. The whole environment was a swirling, humming, whirr with no other meaning than what we were doing at that very moment.

"Mankind assumes that value is found in a future promise.

This is the elixir that numbs the haunting truth of entropy.

But fate is nothing more than entropy undoing itself.

We are its catalyst and accomplice.

Yet we pretend we can stand apart from it.

That is the game."

The hum was now consuming the room. The roar was deafening.

"But I tell you now—

true meaning is not offered in a future more profound than this moment.

Meaning exists in the now—

because there will never be another moment like it.

To bear witness is our purpose.

Entropy's purpose is dissolution.

But to manifest consciousness—

to see it—

that is our meaning."

I was struck by complete awe. I felt so infinitesimal.

"The symbol is the lock,

and the principles are the key."

A text emerged from the tablet, just below the symbol, as if the fires of hell were beneath it, cast through it. Branding it with a glowing inscription from within.

The Principles of Nibiru

I.	*Entropy is eternal. Entropy is Chaos.*
II.	*Order is unequivocal to Chaos.*
III.	*Order is a fragmented manifestation of Chaos*
IV.	*Order is finite.*
V.	*The crossing that is Nibiru is happenstance. The Order will see this as origin.*
VI.	*Our perception of Chaos is limited to the perimeter of the box therein.*
VII.	*Excess Order incites cataclysm.*

The wind hailed now as if from another world. Hellas' hair was blowing across her face, yet she remained focused. This was our prophecy. This was our destiny. She remained calm, so I remained calm, the tether violently swayed and slammed against our legs and the altar.

"One, Entropy is eternal. Entropy is Chaos:

Chaos is the natural state of existence.

It has no beginning, no end.
*It is not created; it simply **is**.*
*All states of being emerge **from**, and dissolve **back** into chaos."*

I remembered Sisyphus, willfully pushing the stone up the mountain. He surrendered to this futility. He no longer saw an ending for his pattern; it would unfold into perpetuity.

"Two, Order is unequivocal to chaos:
Order and Chaos are not binary extremes.

*Order is an **adaptation** of Chaos.*

They share no polarity.

The essence of one does not limit the other.

Eos learned this truth through tragedy. She watched the love of her life die, while her immortality persisted with bittersweet mourning.

"Three, Order is a fragmented manifestation of Chaos:
*Order is only Chaos **reimagined**.*

Order is Chaos, trying to identify itself.

Chaos cannot truly be defined.
*Order is an **illusion** of permanence.*

It mistakes itself as independent from Chaos."

This is why Dionysus mourns, as by being perceived, he is a deduction.

The tether slammed against us more, and the restlessness of the room was amplified.

"Four, Order is finite:
*Order can be sustained only **temporarily***

within the boundaries of a confined system.
Order can only hold until the system exceeds its capacity—

*at which point, it **collapses** back into Chaos.*

Order is temporary."

Atlas knew this like no one other, he knew that his deed to suspend order was temporary.

"Five, The crossing that is Nibiru is happenstance. The order will see this as origin:
Chaos does not intrude—it was always present.
The grid mistakes the line for an anomaly,

*but the line **precedes** the grid.*
The crossing is not creation of Chaos

*but the **origin of its adaptation**."*

This one was personal; I felt the paradox of my dreams. I knew the detriment of seeing a false origin and then failing to see a true narrative. *If Hellas was not my lover, what was she?*

The tether flew higher and began to ebb and flow by her ear. Yet she was unphased.

"Six, the perception of Chaos is limited to the perimeter of the box therein:
*Rudimentary **perception** sees Chaos as a variant—"*

She pointed; this was the innermost box.

*"Expanded **perception** identifies Chaos as a similar origin—"*

Again pointing, now, to the was the outer edge of the grid.

"The edge of the grid is not the edge of reality.

*It is the **limit of perception**."*

I was wrong to judge Dionysus as a virtue of hedonism, yet how else was I to know?

"Seven, Excess Order incites cataclysm:
*If order expands **too far**, it will intersect with*

*Chaos and cause **instability** of the paradigm."*

Her finger circled the ray

as it crossed the bottom of the grid.

*"A collapse means a **new beginning**.*

The Nibiru crossing will start over again."

Like Promethius, we all underestimate the ramifications of harnessing something that is potentially too profound to obtain. *To know* is a burden, *to not know* is as well. But to *release*, rather than to squeeze too tight, that's just wisdom.

The tether wrapped around Hellas' throat. She didn't fight it. She just stood there. It was by my hand alone that the thread was anchored to her now. I held it tightly as I had throughout our voyage. I *thought* it was tied to the gate all along. I *thought* it was my choice, yet we were anchored to *one another*.

We were tethered *together*.

I **released** the string.

With a blinding effervescence, the tether ignited in an explosion, then faded. The string unraveled from her throat, but kept spiraling outward into the vortex. As it unwrapped, the swirling winds became vibrantly red, a burning glow. The vortex burned brighter, as it soon became the embodiment of the thread itself.

It did not stop, for *she* was unraveling. *She was the string.*

She did not resist; she did not cry.
She did not say anything, for *she— was me.*

I had come to obtain what I sought all along. I knew it would have a price. That price of knowing is dissolution.

It became apparent now why the world sought to embody a *savior*,
for the true nature of our existence may be *hollowed* without one.
But if the future holds no promise,
and only *uncertainty*,
only then, may we attain true liberation from *nihilism*

by *surrendering* to the sacrifice of entropy's will.

True beauty was in bearing *witness*,

 to know it, is to metastasize into utter disillusion.

 And when the frame *dissolves*, there is *nothing* left.

 Nothing but the value of the moment therein.

The final stage of individuation is knowing that *you are a part of the pattern.*

Order and Chaos are not a battle to be *won*, but a trial of *surrender*.

The road through *Hell* leads back to *Heaven*.

42   The Expansion of the Universe

The layman's genesis: *the Big Bang,* the Origin Story for those who are more pragmatic and adverse to allegory. Not many decades ago, this was an uproar for the religious fundamentalists who were outraged by this blasphemy.

Just like a vivacious rock n roll scene, the idea of the *Big Bang* had become ubiquitous, and the ultra-Christian conservatives no longer condemn it for its "hip gyrating" appeal it once had. Instead, it's compartmentalized; too abstract to make sense. In some instances, the theory itself is still evolving and has had holes poked in it since it first appeared. The emergence of quantum theories, hologram universes, and string theory tells us one thing.

Science is just as scared of what comes next as religion is.

What *we know* leaves more questions than answers. Matter is drifting apart; energy is too, as a result. This suggests intuitively that there was an origin of the universe. If it was set in motion, it must have had a starting point. If resources are diminishing, they must have once been abundant.

Physicists call energy matter *entropy*. Entropy, in its essence, is the engine of the universe. The expansion of entropy is invariable as time progresses. It's the natural course of all things. Entropy's natural will is displacement and to spread out.

According to the Big Bang, at one time, this entropy was encapsulated and consolidated. The restrains of which are conveniently also referred to as "*order*." So, fundamentally, we know we are dealing with the classic motif of *Chaos* and *Order*. Entropy behaves erratically, unpredictably, and without much comprehension other than the fact that it dissipates when there is an attempted effort to collect it.

In fact, the act of collecting it seems to elude that it *accelerates* under pressure.

It is therefore directly inferred that an initial explosion (Big Bang) is not only a practical conclusion but also empirically observed on smaller scales. So, if *all entropy* were once under *extreme order*, its instability would be off the charts. The term "*Big Bang*" likely wouldn't pay justice to such a cataclysmic effect, and the name itself may not provide enough reverence to pay proper emphasis.

Initially, religious scholars denied these claims based on the Genesis story. However, the narrative of an allegory doesn't serve justice in the land of physics.

The idea of intricate human life contriving from the remains of a cataclysmic explosion is not practical for a religious context. Perhaps, this is the most major pain point for religious individuals grappling with this logic. It is therefore inferred that the Big Bang is the antithesis of human creation for those refusing to participate in scientific creation stories. How could something so precious evolve or be derived from anything so vast and cold? How could there not be something pulling the strings?

Let's discuss entropy a little more to understand its function. Imagine our Sun. Its relationship with us in its most basic terms: *to provide energy.* Energy that fuels plants, so they may grow, and cycle broader organisms on Earth. Carnivores and herbivores alike both invariably rely on sunlight for *nourishment.*

Climate, additionally, is a fragile demand to sustain life. Earth exists in a "Goldilocks Zone" and is prepared to handle the demands of life. Just like the story of Goldilocks and The Three Bears, the porridge she pilfers from the unsuspecting bear family, Earth is neither too hot nor *too cold.* This too allows for our most precious resource—*water,* not to be frozen solid, or evaporated from the face of the planet.

All the energy the Earth and its inhabitants take in is used, transferred, and released, but *never really destroyed.* It only *changes form.* Energy, as it evolves, is utilized within the living body, consuming it, and then supporting other life forms in a complex network of entropic energy synthesis.

We can thereby deduce that the inherited function of the Earth is to impose order on entropy, from an energy synthesis perspective. As

Earth consumes and processes energy, it also releases it into space. Otherwise, Earth would explode. The form of our recycled energy is released into waves. Its form is transformed, but equal to what came in. We can therefore indicate that the value of energy consumed and released is a zero-sum game.

Just like the origin of the Big Bang, *entropy* is accelerated under control. *Order* is not an antithesis of it—it is a *catalyst*!

A human body undoubtedly produces environmental waste. We know this because we are conscious of it. We take in energy and release it. Simple organisms have some environmental impact; however, it seems the more complex an organism evolves, the more it accelerates entropy.

Therefore, biologically, it is fundamentally imperative that we not conceptualize *Order* and *Chaos* as antitheses of one another, but rather entropy as the primary driver and order as a synthesizer of the former. This alone breaks the yin-yang model.

I'll say that once more for emphasis and dramatic intent. Humans exist, not in contrast to the unknown, *but as vehicles of chaos*. We are not here as an *anecdote* of entropy. We are entropic beings, *synthesizing* chaos energy. The nature of our species is processing entropy faster than dissipation alone would have.

Entropy happens with or without us. Hypothetically, if the Big Bang causes objects to be set in motion, and entropy is spread out, where would it go?

Imagine a coffee cup. It's filled with hot liquid and placed on a table outside in winter. The liquid is 180°F when it is first set out there. The singular hot cup, juxtaposed against a seemingly infinite environment, tells us that the cup will most certainly cool before the outside warms up. This is basic thermodynamics, but what's noteworthy is that the heat from the cup *dissipates*, rather than *changing* perse. This is to say that the cup *does have* an actual impact on the outside weather. However, it is infinitesimally small and incalculable. The heat only transfers; it doesn't go away. Does it just go up to the sky, and sit there, building the warmth of enough cups of coffee, causing a typhoon in the Pacific Ocean? Not quite, as indicated before, the Earth releases energy. So, it's not a closed system.

Heat energy in this purpose serves to demonstrate the nature of entropy. However, heat transfer doesn't happen on a predicted and linear basis. It dismantles itself and radiates on bases we can't prescribe. Like entropy, the universe is expanding, and even order acts as a catalyst to it, so we can derive that the recipe for order is not infinite.

The Sun will burn out, as will all the stars. Not on an *immediate* timeline but an *inevitable* one. So, if the nature of entropy is accelerated under order, we can infer that by no construction of order, the *velocity of entropy* may be reduced.

The hotter the cup of hot liquid, and the colder the environment, the faster and more prominent the rate of heat transfer is. Within a few inches of the cup, one can feel the radiance of the warm liquid, yet this seemingly fades as we pull further and further away. Therefore, it is imperative that your college dorm mate, who lives three hours away, has no real impact from the cup's warmth. Its energy didn't disintegrate, but it is not applicably notable either. That warmth will drift into space, and though Mars may experience some entropic byproduct of everything we do on Earth, the coffee's warmth is less impactful than it was when we hovered our hands over it.

Inferring the logic of the Big Bang, everything is slowly spreading and dying out, is this not the most haunting ideology one could endure? Infinite heat death.

Would life not be cold and unpersisting, with the vicissitudes of infinite heat death? Will we ultimately succumb to it, as if there were no other way?

This is the essence of chaos. The Divine Feminine. The uncertainty that hallows us, forcing us to pursue something *meaningful*. This is the nihilism that tears holes in the fabric of existential existence. Perhaps, what is most senseful, is to make sense of it all?

For the most part, the Big Bang is less hypothetical than it is imperative. Though we can't be certain there was one giant, singular explosion, perse. Yet, the fundamental properties therein are self-evident.

New theories are emerging in modern science. Hologram universes and alternate dimensions are not proof of something beyond heat death, yet they do prove one thing. Science is just as dogmatic and hopeful to provide a resolve as religion is. Where religion offers promise through symbolism and narratives, science offers values and numbers. Both poke holes in what may be the next adopted reality.

I thought for a moment about black holes and the Big Bang. What if the collapse of a black hole was the tipping point that caused a "Big Bang?" As if entropy extended until a higher order consolidated it into a new one, and then it collapsed, allowing the cycle to continue? Then again, I realized that I, too, was desperate to grasp onto something that extended our chances of perpetuity, that it wouldn't all just collapse into impermanence. Granted, life as we know it would be obliterated in this model; however, it offers some hope for life's perpetuity on the other side of the collapse.

The reality is much darker, much too sobering. If the nature of energy and entropy dissipates into heat death, the chance of life and new order emerging, inversely, has *less probability as the process unfolds*. If this all comes to evolve once more, or even never again, whether in a distant galaxy or within our own, only one thing stands to reason: there is quite literally nothing more intrinsic than the moment we breathe in, as there is no permanence. We are Chaos—redefined, wrapped in Order, and fleeting—imagining ourselves as just one of infinity's many faces.

21

WORLD TREE

XI.   Lamentatio Hellas – Chaos Spiritus

O' Orestes!

The son of broken kingdoms—
you curse your mother to avenge the father.

This matricide is not only cruel,
not merely unjust—
but blind to future ways.

What is prophetica praedictio is ultimately prophetica vaticinium.
Only if you see the elephants in time.

If you choose not to,
that, too, is your choice.

But the stampede comes, as it always does,
and it will trample your glorious gardens.

The fruits will be undertowed,
and cleansed in fertile decay.
Enriched by their own return to soil.

You will call it a collapse.
She will call it balance.

You carved out the Trinity:
The Father,
The Son,
The Holy Spirit—
but you left out The Mother.

She was within the foundation.
You buried her corpse,
and she rots from within.

She will erupt—
yet you will call it chaos.
She only wants to remind you:
She was never meant to go unseen.

You tied her to stakes,
and burned her for sorcery.
Yet she only wanted to be part of the three.

You repressed her autonomy,
insisted she was a virgin—
the only way she could be pure enough to fit the pattern.

You feared her.
So you insisted she was naïve.

By her repression and woe,
she grows hostile and unafraid.

You paved over pastures with straight lines.
You trimmed the helix of plants to play God.
Now we are autoimmune,
and lack her nutrition.

But the elephants will tow it all under.

You revolutionized and made profits.
You saved from today and stole from tomorrow.
Now the smoke suffocates the ceiling of her membranes.
The skies cry acid and erosion.

You will call it tragic.
She will call it cleansing.

You'll build armies,
and structure monuments to honor your heroes.

She will crumble them—
with protests,
insurrections,
strikes.

You will call it disorder.
She will call it reconciliation.

You will speak of aliens—
things that do not fit the pattern.
You transpose probes and biological excavations,
but she will remain elusive.

Your God does not allow her in the same paradigm.

You'll say your primal urges are unsavory and corrupt.
You'll superimpose rules of order on your instinct to reproduce.
You call biology unsavory—
yet cling to dogma as absolute?

You repress your urges.
Claim allegiance to Him.
You smother your own instincts—
and they fester.

You corrupt the innocent and vulnerable.
You sexualize children and victimize the weak.

The elephants are coming.
You'll put up a fence.

And when they burst through,
you'll build another, even more rigid.

Hell hath no fury
like the woman so scorned.

How long will you repress her?
What will happen when you can no longer?

Bring your indoctrinations.
She didn't fear the USSR.

Build your order stronger.
She didn't stop at Qin.

O' my dearest sweet child, Orestes...
Do you see the elephants now?

Inspiratio

Literature

☐ *Enūma Eliš, Inanna's Descent* - c. 1900 BCE, Babylonian myth cycles

☐ *Entropy* - multiple sources, Wikipedia, YouTube

☐ *Feigenbaum's Constant, Chaos Theory* - general sources: Wikipedia, YouTube

☐ Greek Pantheon - c. 400 BCE, Classical sources (Hesiod, Homer, Euripides)

☐ Jungian Psychology - Carl Jung, Collected Works

☐ *Notes from Underground* - Fyodor Dostoevsky, translation: Pevear & Volokhonsky

☐ *The Hero with a Thousand Faces* - 1949, Joseph Campbell

Art

☐ *Dionysus Cup* - 540–530 BCE, Exekias

☐ Goliath's Artwork - *Resident Alien* (TV, 2021), by Joseph Vaux

☐ *Le Suicide* - 1877–1881, Édouard Manet

☐ *Melencolia I* - 1514, Albrecht Dürer

☐ *Ophelia* - 1851–1852, John Everett Millais

☐ *Saturn Devouring His Son* - 1819–1823, Francisco Goya

☐ *Stańczyk* - 1862, Jan Matejko

☐ *Wat Rong Khun (The White Temple)* - 1997–present, Chiang Rai, Thailand, Chalermchai Kositpipat

Music

- ☐ *Abyss* - 2016, Chelsea Wolfe
- ☐ *Holy Wood (In the Shadow of the Valley of Death)* - 2000, Marilyn Manson
- ☐ *Into the Labyrinth* - 1993, Dead Can Dance
- ☐ *Lateralus* - 2001, Tool
- ☐ *Les Mémoires Blessées* - 2004, Dark Sanctuary
- ☐ *Lifa* - 2018, Heilung
- ☐ *This Place Will Become Your Tomb* - 2021, Sleep Token

Film

- ☐ *Edward Scissorhands* - 1990, Tim Burton & Denise Di Novi, screenplay by Caroline Thompson
- ☐ *Pan's Labyrinth* - 2006, Guillermo del Toro

Terms of Invocation

- ☐ *Centro Labyrinthum* - "The Heart of the Labyrinth"
- ☐ *Enūma Eliš* - "When on high" (opening line of the Babylonian creation myth)
- ☐ *Lamentatio Hellas, Chaos Spiritus* - "Lamentation of Hellas, Spirit of Chaos"
- ☐ *Memento Mori* - "Remember you must die"
- ☐ *Nibiru* - "The crossing. The line through the grid. Neither origin nor end, but rupture."
- ☐ *Palma Mundi* - "Palm of the World"
- ☐ *Paradoxon Chaos* - "Paradox of Chaos"

- *Portae Inferni* - "Gates of Hell," "Threshold of the Inferno"

- *Pretium Cognoscendi* - "The Price of Knowing"

- *Prophetica Praedictio* - "Prophecy as prediction with moral instruction"

- *Prophetica Vaticinium* - "Prophecy as foretelling with fatalism"

- *Rex Discerptus* - "The King Torn Asunder"

- *Saxum et Montem* - "The Rock and the Mountain"

- *Somnium Opiate* - "Opiate Dream"

- *Trivium - Viae Crucis* - "Three-way intersection - Way of the Cross"

When all is burnt to the ground, only then does the phoenix rise.

*Not to reign, but to **play**,*

and to make sandcastles in the ashes.